ISBN: 978-0-244-13734-2

14 BATTLES FOR THE WHITE RACE

By Adam Richards

ISBN: 978-1-312-97300-8

Introduction

Many of our fair people have been force fed a fictitious account of world history that singles out the White race as the sole practitioner of slavery, genocide and a long list of other so-called crimes. Almost none of today's history books describe any of the many non-white invasions of Europe as acts of racist aggression. So many members of our White race have had their brains polluted with such a large amount of this biased junk history that a lot of them have already pled guilty for the crime of being the descendants if history's bad guys. This feeling of guilt in White people has made many of them believe that they are somehow responsible for the plight of their historical enemies, and they are quite literally killing themselves to try to "make things right".

The texts that are contained in this booklet were written with the intent to share an account of well known historical events that are looked at from the White man's point of view. A French Canadian White activist was the first person to print some of these texts for distribution, and it was his idea to put 14 of them in this booklet. He is a real life fighter for the 14 words, and I'll always be grateful to him for his assistance. It is a true honor to call him a comrade.

I am a proud member of the Creator Skinheads (CSH), and the 11th aim of our organization is: "to promote the best interests of the White race through positive and legal means." It is hoped that the best interests of the White race will be promoted in some small way by the distribution of this booklet. Inside of it our people can find the facts that prove that our heroic White ancestors are not history's bad guys. The suicidal belief of White guilt must be replaced with a feeling of White hot hatred for those whose ancestors did all that they could in the past to destroy our race, because the mud races are fighting hard to exterminate our fair people today.

The enemies of the White race are shown no respect in this booklet. Many of the texts inside of it are about battles that were fought bitterly for the survival and advancement of the White race. A lot of the texts in this booklet have hard earned lessons that we can learn from as well as examples of courage to inspire us in battles yet to come.

Ben Klassen said it best in Nature's Eternal Religion. "*Our first objective in this battle is, and must be, to unite the White Man, and straighten out his thinking. United and organized the White race is ten times as powerful as the rest of the world combined. Once we have done this, the Jew and the nigger problem is as good as solved.*" I, 2, p. 26

RaHoWa!

Marathon 490 BC

The battle of Marathon was the first major engagement fought by our White race for the defense of our living space in Europe. Some of our Indo-European ancestors founded a powerful Empire in the east, but they had absorbed whole nations of mud peoples in the process. Another group of our White forefathers settled in Greece, and many of them were determined to keep the Eastern hordes from drowning our flourishing Western civilization in mud. The Greeks were both militarily and politically weaker than their enemies. So, they had to rely on bold tactics and raw courage to even the unfavorable odds that they were up against. In the up close, and violent fighting that took place in this battle thousands were killed. Many of our people today don't even realize that they pay tribute to this bloody event every year. Therefore, it is very important for all of our White racial comrades to learn about the battle of Marathon that was fought to protect our White civilization.

Long ago, in what is today the modern day country of Iran, our ancien White ancestors founded the powerful Persian Empire. They went on to conquer many non-White peoples in areas as far east as India, and as far west as turkey. Even the half breed niggers of Egypt were subjugated by Persia's might, but sadly many of these peoples were brought into the Persian Empire's administration as well as its army.

In modern day Greece, which is located in

Southeastern Europe, another group of our ancestors who called themselves Hellens founded great city states on the mainland as well as on the surrounding islands. They also had settlements on Turkey's west coast, and they called Western Turkey "Iona". Greece was called "Hellas", and the time period between 800 BC and 400 BC is known as the "Hellenic Golden Age". A vast amount of our knowledge about architecture, art, philosophy, math and science can be traced back to this period. The ancient civilization of the Hellens was truly beautiful in every sense of the word.

The Persian Empire was founded in the sixth century, and it didn't take long for its unstoppable army to conquer Iona. However, the White men of Iona launched a defiant rebellion in 499 BC. The city state of Athens sent their White Ionian brothers some help from European mainland, and this act of support enraged the Persian Emperor Darius the Great. It took the Persians five long years to crush White resistance in Iona, and Darius was so mad after it ended that he decided to send his interracial hordes to enslave the people of Hellas. Then the path would be clear for all of Europe to be dragged down into the mud.

In 490 BC Darius sent a general named Datis with a multiracial army of 25,000 infantry and 1,00 cavalry to invade our White race's living space in Europe. Datis divided this force into two and sent 10,000 soldiers to destroy the Hellen city of Eritia. He landed his other 15,000 infantry and 1,000 cavalry by ship at the plain of Marathon about 26 miles from Athens. When the Hellens learned of the locations of the invasion forces they sent 10,000 Athenian and Plataeain infantry under the command of a man named Callimachus to the plain of Marathon. They got there just in time to position themselves on the high ground before the invaders could begin their march inland.

The Hellens did not want to give up their small advantage by leaving their superior position and the invaders did not want to attack the Hellens on the high ground. Eight days went by without any fighting, but time was not on the Hellens' side. There were some among them who thought that Hellas should bow down and surrender to the Persian Empire. The Hellens would also become even more outnumbered than they already were if the Persians were given enough time to unite their two forces, they voted on what action to take, and they were so divided that it all came down to Callimachus's final decision. When Callimachus heard that Eritra had fallen, he gave the order to attack!

A warrior named Militiades was one of the Hellens who had experience fighting the Persian army, and he came forward with a bold plan of attack. Callimachus wisely gave him free reign to put his plan into action, so Militiades ordered the center of the Hellen phalanx to be thinned down to four rows of infantry from its usual eight rows. He then used these extra troops to deepen his flanks from their usual eight rows to twelve rows. On September 21ˢᵗ the Persian cavalry rode a mile away to a marsh to get water. So on this day in 490 BC the White men of Europe began marching towards the invaders at a steady pace.

None of the Hellens were archers, so they were armed with spears, swords and shields. They knew that the Persians were going to shoot thousands of arrows at them as they advanced, and that they would have nothing to fight back with. So, in order to minimize the effect of the Persian archers, the Hellens didn't start running until they got inside of the 200yard range of the enemy's bows. The valiant Hellens charged through the hail of missiles and only a few men were hit. Then the one mile long Hellen phalanx slammed into the Persians and their mud auxiliaries!

The Persians pushed back against the center of the Hellen phalanx and the Hellens fell back to the high ground where they had started their advance from. While this was happening the reinforced flanks of the Hellen phalanx began to push the flanks of the invasion force inward. The Hellens in the center were now bitterly holding their ground, and the enemy was soon enveloped by the Hellen flank assault! Militiades's plan had worked out great, because the invaders were now getting slaughtered! They quickly began to run for their sorry lives back to their ships but Callimachus personally led the Hellens after them. He died a hero's death near the enemy ships while stabbing at those who had arrogantly dared to think that they could conquer the land of Hellas! About 192 other Hellens died with Callimachus but they took 6,400 of their hated foes down with them…

A runner named Pheidippides was sent to deliver the news of victory to Athens, and he ran the 26 miles so fast that it is said he died from exhaustion after reporting the news. This is where the tradition of the Marathon race comes from, so in a way our people are still paying tribute to this great event almost 2,500 years later. Pheidippides was soon followed by the triumphant army in order to protect Athens from the remaining 19,600 invaders traveling by ship. The Persian commander took one look at the blood stained Hellens waiting for round two and decided to retreat back to Asia when he saw them at Athens.

If things had gone differently our White race's gene pool could have been destroyed by the waves of muds that would have been used by the Persians to conquer Hellas as well as all of Europe. A lot of valuable knowledge that has been passed on to us from the Ancient Greeks would have been lost too. This is why this battle that was the first of many major battles fought to protect European soil should be celebrated forever.

This monumental event marked the beginning of our White race's courageous struggle to defend our living space in Europe from those who want to mongrelize our fair people. Our Persian ancestors made the age old mistake of absorbing non-Whites into their living space, and they wanted to pull us down into their mud puddle. Our Ancient

Greek ancestors, who helped lay the foundations for what we call Western civilization, saved the Whites in Europe from suffering a dark fate under the Persians. This underdog victory is a tactical masterpiece that was pulled off by brave White men. All of this is why we should honor this battle in which the men of the West stopped an invasion from the East on the plain of Marathon, so our people could live to fight another day.

Salamis 480 BC

Salamis is the first decisive naval battle in our White race's history. In 481 BC The Persian Empire set out to invade Ancient Greece for the second time in less than 10 years. The Greeks, who called themselves Hellens, had no way of putting together an army big enough to stop the gigantic horde of mongrels from overrunning their land. However, many White men from Hellas would die bravely while trying to stop what many believed to be the unstoppable, and they won immortality for their attempt. This was a brutal struggle between white and darkness that called for ruthless action to be taken. In the end the fate of our fair people was forced into the hands of a small number of White sailors surrounded by a huge enemy fleet in the water off the coast of an island called Salamis.

Xerces, the son of Darius the Great, rallied an army of hundreds of thousands of muds and niggers together in 481 BC to do what his father had failed to do in 490 BC. His goal was to subjugate Ancient Greece as well as all the land that was west of it under the Persian Empire. He had a great bridge built out of boats between Southern Europe and modern day Turkey to allow his multi-racial army to march over the narrow sea that separates Europe from Asia. A fleet of 1,400 ships sailed along the coast to support the army. The Persian Empire was still mostly ruled by Whites, but at this time in its history it was in a downward spiral towards mongrelization.

The Hellens of Ancient Greece were divided into city states that fought each other all the time, but many of them joined forces when they learned about the approaching hordes of Persia. They were still vastly outnumbered though, so the odds of the Hellens stopping the invasion of their land were slim to none. Nevertheless the Ancient Greeks were some of the finest White racial specimens that have ever lived. Therefore, it is not surprising that 5,000 Hellens marched towards the oncoming invasion to give it a go.

The defenders were led by a hardcore group of 300 Hellens from the city state of Sparta and their king Leonidas. They positioned themselves in a pass called Thermopylae where they believed they could hold back the hundreds of thousands of invaders. These heroes held their ground for three days of ferocious fighting! Sadly, their flank was exposed to the enemy by a traitor named Ephiates. Leonidas and his 300 Spartans won immortality in this engagement for voluntarily fighting to the death, so their comrades could escape. Xerxes was enraged by this defiant act, because it cost his army over 20,000 men!

While history was being made at Thermopylae there was a fleet of 300 Hellen ships fighting the invaders at sea. A great storm hit the Persian fleet, and had destroyed 400 of its ships. However, this still left the enemy with 1,000 vessels! This fact did not stop the White sailors from attacking the invaders though. The little White fleet actually attacked the huge Persian navy twice! Their ships were slower than the ones that the Persians had so it is shocking to learn that the Hellens were able to hold their own against them. They only disengaged from the invaders after they heard about the Persian army's breakthrough at Thermopylae. At this time the Athenians in the fleet convinced the other Hellens to sail south, and help them evacuate their city before the invaders got to it.

The Hellen fleet was now in the small area of sea between the coastlines of Athens and the Island of Salamis off Greece's western coast. It was under the overall command of a Spartan named Eurybiades, but many of the Hellens were now asking him to allow them to return to their individual cities to save their families from the Persian army now overrunning their land. The Athenian ships made up the majority of the Hellen fleet, and they were led by a farsighted man named Themistocles who knew that the only way to save his people on land was to destroy their enemies on the sea. He needed to force the Hellen fleet to stay together though, and he did this by sending a secret message to the Persians that promised the surrender of the Athenian ships if they attacked the Hellens right now.

On September 23rd 480 BC, four months after the invasion began, the Persians took Themistocles's bait, and advanced towards the Hellen fleet. They sent a force of half breed niggers from Egypt around the other side of Salamis to cut off the

Hellens only escape route. While their other main force of about 1,000 ships moved in for the kill…

All of the Hellen ships pulled away from the enemy at first, but then one lone ship full of courageous White men lunged towards the huge invasion fleet! It plunged right into the enemy formation, and rammed the first ship it came into contact with. This bold act inspired the rest of the Hellen fleet to attack as well, and the Persians couldn't back away fast enough! The enemy's faster ships had nowhere to move to in the narrow sea that Themistocles had lured them into, so the White men's heavy ships began to smash into them!

Many of the White warriors began jumping onto the enemy's ships to kill the muds and niggers in close combat! The White Persians who had tried to force the White race into a multiracial mud puddle were cut down next to their nigger comrades! It went on like this for about 8 hours as the water turned red with the blood of White Europe's enemies. Xerxes had a front row seat to all this, so he got to watch as the biggest navy ever assembled was torn to pieces.

The world was turned upside down after this battle! Xerxes's mongrel army still outnumbered any force that the Hellens could throw at it, but his will to fight was broken with his ships in the sea off the coast of Salamis. He knew that the Hellens could now send their victorious little fleet to destroy the boat bridge between Europe and Asia. This fact filled Xerxes with fear, and it drove him to return to Asia a few days after the battle. His army that he left behind in Greece was annihilated in the battle of Plataea about a year later. It had about 180,000 soldiers in it, but it was no match for the 80,000 Hellens who were inspired by the valiant actions of their brothers at Thermopylae and Salamis!

The battle of Salamis was an important event, because it stopped the invasion of Greece dead in its tracks! This victory insured the survival of the beautiful civilization of Ancient Greece so it could become a foundation block of the West. It kept the Persian's mongrel hordes out of Europe and this made it possible for other White peoples like the Romans to carry the torch for our race in the future.

Salamis is the first naval victory in world history to decide the outcome in one of the wars that our people fought to protect their land in. No one in the Persian army thought that their hundreds of thousands of soldiers could be stopped by a little fleet of 300 ships! The Hellens of Ancient Greece were a unique people who proved over and over again the value of quality over quantity. They set the bar high when the 300 Spartans gave their lives so their brothers could live to fight another day. It all came down to the seafaring skills of a small number of White warriors though. Men like Themistocles used guile when courage wasn't enough to get the job done, and the multiracial invasion was broken on the prows of Hellen ships!

Metaurus River 207 BC

Our endangered White race can learn a lot from the way the battle of Metaurus river and the Punic wars were fought. The Carthaginians were on a mission in the third century BC to achieve world domination, but the Romans were not going to just meekly bow down to them. So Carthage instigated a war to bring Rome to its knees by force! Thus, the Romans found themselves in a desperate situation that only a bold plan of action could get them out of, so they put it all on the line at the battle of Metaurus river. This battle inspired the Romans to continue to embrace an "all or nothing" mind set that fueled them to finally destroy their enemies once and for all! I believe the victory or death mentality that the Romans displayed in the battle of Metaurus river can, and should be embraced by our people today in the struggle that we are in if they want to win.

The Carthaginians were originally an Old Mediterranean European people known as Phoenicians who settled in modern day Lebanon in 2700 BC. Their seafaring skills earned them a dominant position in world trade, but this led to an unhealthy amount of contact with non-White peoples. They absorbed a significant amount of Semitic blood into their gene pool over the centuries, but they never really stopped showing some of the White characteristics associated with our noble White race. Carthage was founded by them in 800 BC where the modern day city of Tunis stands today. A lot of their other cities were lost in the many wars that they fought, so the Phoenicians became known as the Carthaginians after their great city became the center of their power. By the third century BC these white skinned Semites had the Mediterranean Sea and many of its islands in a choke hold.

Some of our White ancestors living in the Mediterranean area founded the city of Rome in 753 BC. By 270 BC they absorbed all of their White cousins who lived on the Italian peninsula with them into a great White nation. The Romans were highly skilled organizers, and valiant warriors who built a great civilization of their own upon the foundations that had been laid down by the Ancient Greeks as well as other White peoples. They had no intention of falling under the yoke of Carthage's growing power that was moving inland from the sea. So Rome built a navy of its own, and wrestled control of the European island of Sicily from Carthage after defeating the "Punics" (Latin word for Phoenicians) in 241 BC.

After getting defeated by the Romans in what became known as the first "Punic War" the Carthaginians invaded Spain in 237. It is a well known fact that Cartage's armies were made up of the best battle hardened mercenaries that money could buy and that they were led by talented Carthaginian officers. Therefore, the Whites living in Spain, without an organized military to fight back with, fell under Carthage's rule. The overall commander of Carthage's mercenaries was a very distinctively White looking man named Hannibal Barca who decided to provoke another war with Rome in 219 BC by besieging a pro Roman Spanish town called Saguntum that he knew Rome would go to war for.

Hannibal marched up out of Spain, through Southern France (Gaul), over the Alps, and down into Italy with tens of thousands of well trained White mercenaries. He then defeated the Romans in battle after battle for 12 years! Hannibal beat the Roman people to the ground, but they bitterly refused to let their capital fall into his hands. The indefatigable Romans fought a war of attrition under the guidance of Fabius Cunctator with the intent to bleed Hannibal's army dry until he had no choice but to withdraw.

The Roman people's fanatical resistance to Hannibal's occupation of their land drove him to conclude that the city of Rome had to be taken. However, Hannibal needed more mercenaries, so he sent orders to his brother Hasdruble to bring reinforcements to him. Hasdruble arrived in Northern Italy in 207 BC with 50,000 men and got things started by putting the city of Placentia under siege. The people of Placentia were just as stubborn as the rest of the Romans though, so Hasdruble abandoned the siege to march south. He then discovered a Roman army in his path led by a man named Livius Salinator. At this time Hasdruble sent two messages to Hannibal requesting to join their two armies together in Umbria province.

These messages were intercepted on their

way to Hannibal's camp at Canusium (Canoia) by the Roman army that was shadowing Hannibal's forces. This Roman army was led by Caius Claudius Nero, and he decided to gamble the fate of his people on a plan that no one had tried before. He ordered a small number of his soldiers to keep watching Hannibal's positions and then he began to march towards Hasdruble with 7,000 of his best legionaries!

Nero's men covered 200 miles and joined forces with Livius's army in only 7 days! Hasdruble found out that the Romans were up to something, so he tried to march his army up the Via Flaminia to get away from them. His native Italian guides deserted him though and this forced the Carthaginian commander to fight where he now stood next to the Metaurus river, which is probably the modern day Ravine of San Angelo. Hasdruble broke his army up into three formations. The one that made up his army's northern flank was facing the river, while the center formation as well as the southern flank formation that he had personal command of had their backs to the river of the eastern side of it.

The Romans positioned themselves in three formations as well. Livius commanded the one facing Hasdruble's formation, the center Roman formation was commanded by the practor Porcius and Nero's men positioned themselves on the southern Roman flank across the Metaurus river from the white mercenaries holding the enemy's left flank. The fighting began right away and Porcius's men holding the center as well as Livius's soldiers on the left found themselves in a vicious engagement with the invaders. While this was happening Nero was discovering that his men and the White mercenaries on the other side couldn't do any real arm to each other.

Nero knew that the Romans had to defeat Hasdruble by any means necessary! Anything less than total victory would allow the two Carthaginian armies to unite and then capture Rome. So, Nero brazenly led the bulk of his elite legionaries southward around the back of the other two Roman formations and then charged into Hasdruble's flank! The invaders were then enveloped, and annihilated!

As soon as the fighting stopped Nero led his exhausted warriors on another 200 mile forced march back to reunite with the few that were still watching Hannibal as he waited to hear back from his brother. Hannibal had no idea that Nero had ever been gone, and he only found out after a Roman cavalryman rode up close to his camp to throw a sack into it before riding away. When Hannibal opened the sack he knew right away that no reinforcements were coming. Hannibal had beaten the Romans for 12 years straight, but all he had to show for it all was his brother's head in a bag…

Hasdruble was forced into the battle of Metaurus river before he was able to join up with Hannibal because Nero was willing to do anything he had to do in order to defeat his people's enemies. Nero's aggressiveness was contagious, and a Roman army commanded by Scipio was later sent to North

Africa to take the fight to the enemy's homeland! This force Hannibal to retreat from Italy to go home, and defend his own capital. In 202, the second Punic war ended after Hannibal was defeated by Scipio's legionaries at the battle of Zama. Rome's offensive attitude did not go away after the war ended though. In fact a Roman known as Cato the Elder ended all of his speeches in the senate with the words "Delenda Est Carthago!" (Carthage must be destroyed). Many years later Carthage started the third Punic war by attacking one of Rome's allies and Carthage was destroyed in 146 BC.

Today our whole White race is being attacked by a nation of White skinned Semites who have the best mercenaries money can buy to protect them. When our people try to fight back against these Jews they are smashed by the mostly White policemen and soldiers of the so-called "Western governments" that these Jews control. Nevertheless, I believe we should strive to emulate Nero's tenacious will to keep fighting and take any opportunity that comes our way to hurt our enemies no matter what risk we have to take to do it. Just like Cato the Elder we must also commit ourselves to destroying our enemies no matter how long it takes!

We can learn a lot form the way the indomitable people of Rome won the battle of Metaurus river and the seemingly never ending struggle with Carthage. The Carthaginians were determined adversaries, but the Romans never backed down! They instinctively knew in their hearts that eternal struggle is the price of survival, so they kept fighting no matter how many battles they lost to Hannibal. Nero's bold tactical decision to leave Hannibal practically unguarded to march 200 miles and defeat Hasdruble was the first time in recorded world history that a commander positioned between two enemy armies had ever attempted to attack one before the other could come to its aid. I believe that the words in the 36th Creative Credo of the White Man's Bible explain the moral of this story best, so I will end with them…

"Our fight against the Jews must be the same ultimate goal as Cato the Elder proclaimed repeatedly in the fight against Carthage – Our battle cry must be: Delenda Est Judaica!"

The battle of Chalons-sur-Marne

The battle of Chalons-sur-Marne is one of the greatest victories in European history. It took place in Gaul in AD 451. The men of Europe came together to defend their homeland from the Huns who had put the city of Orleans under siege. When the fighting started, the Huns attacked with everything they had and broke through the Europeans' center. The Europeans' flank was exposed for the Huns to destroy. However, just when all hope was lost, the Europeans counterattacked and won the battle. Western Europe was saved from the Hun invaders and the men of Europe proved that the Huns were not unstoppable.

The battle of Chalons-sur-Marne was fought in AD 451 on the Catalonian fields south of Mery-sur-Seine in the land of Gaul. Today this land is the nation of France and it's located in Western Europe. It is right above Spain and just below Belgium.

This land had been a part of the Roman Empire for a while and a great man named Flavius Aetius was the military commander of this part of the Roman Empire under Emperor Valentinian III. The Romans were a virtuous and industrious Italic people but because of an influx of mud peoples their empire was no longer strong enough to defend all of its lands. However the Romans were still brave and their army had many courageous Celtic warriors from Gaul ready to fight. Aetius took no chances though and he put aside the small differences between his people and the Visigoths in order to make an alliance with them. They were a vigorous and noble Germanic people, who founded a kingdom in Gaul in AD 418. Their great leader was King Theodoric I, son of Alaric. All of these Europeans came together and marched toward the Huns in order to protect their land and families.

The Huns were nomadic and warlike Asian people who began to invade Eastern Europe in AD 372 and Central Europe by AD 450. At this time they were led by a man named Attila who the people of Europe called the "scourge of God". He and 40 000 Huns invaded Western Europe next and put Orleans under siege.

On June 14th the Europeans came to the rescue and saved the city of Orleans. The Huns began to pull back as soon as they saw that the men of the West had united and come to fight. Attila led his men away to the Catalonian fields. On June 20th he stopped and prepared his Huns for battle.

The Huns attacked first and launched a powerful cavalry charge at the center of the European line. Aetius held the left side of the line like a rock against the right wing of the Hun charge but the center was broken through and the Huns began to turn their horses around for a flank attack.

The Germanic Visigoth saw the flank attack coming and sent their reserves into the battle just in time. Just when the Huns thought they were going to win, King Theodoric I, son of Alaric, and his Visigoth horsemen charged and crashed into the Huns. He died a warrior's death in combat and gave his life for his people. His son stepped up and took his father's place right away. Thorismond continued to lead the Visigoths as they killed the invaders side by side with their European brothers from Rome and Gaul. Attila had no choice but to retreat from the battlefield.

The Huns suffered heavy losses in this defeat and the only thing they wanted to do now was escape Western Europe with their lives. Aetius and Thorismond let them get away and the Huns launched one more semi-successful raid against Italy in the South of Europe. Attila died the next year though and the huns were no longer strong enough to hold any lands in Europe thus, they were forced to go back to Asia. Men like Aetius and Theodoric had fought and died for their people and they also showed them that the Huns were not unstoppable.

The battle of Chalons-sur-Marne is one of the European people's greatest victories. It was won on the Catalonian fields of Gaul in Western Europe and is now the modern day nation of France. The Romans and Visigoths came together to defend their lands from the so-far unstoppable Huns. They freed the surrounded city of Orleans and forced the Huns back to the Catalonian fields where they faced the invaders in battle. The Huns came at them in a cavalry charge that broke right through the European battle line at the center. Attila then turned his Huns around to finish off the European Army with a flank attack. however, Theodoric I, King of the Visigoths, launched a cavalry charge of his own that was so strong it smashed the Huns to pieces and won the battle. This united force of European warriors checked the Hun invasion of the West. The Asians never fully recovered from this defeat and they were forced to retreat from all of Europe a few years later. Our European forefathers gave us a great demonstration of what we can do when we work together as one people. We can stop the unstoppable!

Constantinople 717-718 AD

The 8th century battle of Constantinople affected our White race for hundreds of years after it was fought. A fairly new religion called Islam had organized the muds of Arabia against White Christian Europe. The city of Constantinople was the southeastern doorway into our living space in Europe at this time, and bold action was needed to defend it. Overwhelming numbers of men and material came out of Asia to take Constantinople. The White men holding the city refused to go down easy, though. Some of the most critical moments in this fight took place at sea. Logistics played a critical role in this battle, as well. No matter how bad things got, the White men defending Constantinople never lost their will to attack. In the end, they did whatever it took to destroy the Muslim muds on both land and sea. This heroic event prolonged the resistance of our people living in southeastern Europe for centuries.

Islam was founded by a Semitic Arab known as "Mohammed the Prophet", but many believe that his Semitic Jewish wife gave him the real foundation for his religion. Anyways, after Mohammed died in 632 AD it took less than a hundred years for this new religion to unite all the mud peoples of the Middle East and North Africa against the White race in Europe. They tried for the first time to take Constantinople in 674. This first attempt failed, but the muds then went on to invade our race's lands in Spain. By 717 they were again ready to enslave our people in southeastern Europe in the name of their religion, so their new Caliph (religious leader) Suleiman sent the mongrel hordes of Islam to smash the city that stood in their way.

The city of Byzantium was built by the White Romans right on the southeastern tip of Europe alongside the narrow sea that connects the Black Sea to the Mediterranean Sea, and separates Europe from Asia. When the first Christian emperor Constantine made it his capital of the eastern half of the Roman Empire in 330 AD it began to be called Constantinople. After the fall of the Roman people, and the western half of their empire, the eastern half became known as the "Byzantine Empire". This city was now ruled by a minority of White Greeks, and its soldiers were mostly Germanic mercenaries. These White men were all that were holding this old Roman city together. A man named Conon led the Empire's army in modern-day Turkey as it carried out a bitter fighting withdrawal against the advancing Muslim hordes. When he arrived at Constantinople he brazenly pushed the weak-willed Emperor Anastasias aside, and took the crown. Now known as Leo III, he went to work and oversaw the city's preparation for the battle he knew was coming.

The army of Muds was under the command of a man named Musiama, and it was over 80,000 men strong. He planned to use 30,000 of his men to keep an eye on the Asiatic Bulgars near Adrianople, who were also invading Europe, while the majority of his men stormed over Constantinople's walls. The muds also had a fleet of 1,800 ships that they planned to use to cut off the city's supply lines from the ports of both the Black Sea and the Mediterranean Sea. These naval forces were under the command of a man named Suleiman. The mud army crossed over the narrow sea into Europe in July of 717.

They went into action right away, and 50,000 Muslim mongrels crashed into Constantinople's walls. The White men defending the city fought desperately to hold back the assault waves. White heroism won the day, and the muds were successfully thrown back with heavy losses. After this Muslim failure, Musiama decided that a frontal assault on the city's walls was no longer a good idea.

Half of Suleiman's fleet blockaded the approach from the Mediterranean, and the other half set out to blockade the approach from the Black Sea, as well. However, the muds failed to properly navigate the swift currents of the sea in this area, and they were not able to keep their ships in a combat formation. The heavy chain that closed the city's harbor, known as the Golden Horn, was immediately lowered, and the White navy sprang into attack! These sailors were armed with an ancient form of napalm known as "Greek fire", and it did catastrophic damage to the disorganized muds. This ingenious White weapon destroyed so many of Suleiman's ships in this attack that he was unable to cut off the city's supply lines from the Black Sea.

All of the muds' plans had failed at this point, and a period of inaction followed. Then they received some bad news from the home front. Their Caliph, Suleiman, had died from overeating, and the new Caliph was Omar II. He was not a great military mind or anything close to one. As the muds camped outside of the city, and did nothing, the snows began to fall. Winter had come, and many thousands of Muslims died in the winter months. Their supply lines failed to provide them with the logistical support they needed, so their siege of Constantinople did not go too well. All the muds could do was keep sending calls for men and supplies.

In the spring, 400 more ships arrived from Egypt with 50,000 reinforcements, and in a nighttime maneuver this force placed itself in a position to cut off the supplies coming into the city from the Black Sea. So, Constantinople was now under a full land and naval blockade. The city would have to surrender if it stayed that way too long. Then, in June the White navy struck this new part of the Muslim fleet like a thunderstorm, and Greek fire was once again blown into the muds' ships. This surprise attack was another disaster for the Muslims, and it was quickly followed by another on the Asian side of the sea, where more muds were burned alive. These back-to-back defeats at sea devastated the majority of the Muslim's fleet, and it put a violent end to any chance of starving Constantinople into surrendering.

There was another surprise that caught the muds off guard on land, as well. Leo III ruthlessly bribed the Asiatic Bulgars to attack the Muslim army, so they smashed through the force at Adrianople. They then hammered into the Muslims besieging Constantinople. The White men stationed on the city's walls must have really enjoyed watching their Bulgar enemies fighting against their Arab enemies. After this turn of events, the Muslims had a broken army to go with their broken navy! When Omar II learned of all this he himself was broken, as well, and he sent orders for Muslama to retreat! So, the muds were sent back into Asia on August 17th, 718 with what was left of their forces.

This was not just any defeat for the forces of Islam. The battles they had lost in the past were only minor setbacks. In this one, though, they had brought about 210,000 men and over 2,000 ships! Only 30,000 of these traumatized muds and 5 of their scarred ships made it back to Asia! They had never been so utterly beaten down like this by anyone before. It would take many centuries for them to gain the power and knowledge they would need to take Constantinople. If they had been able to take it in 717 they could have made their way deep into Europe without running into anyone strong enough to stop them. Only the Franks of Western Europe were organized into a force large enough to put up a fight, but if the Franks were caught between Arab invasions from both Spain and the east, they may have been overwhelmed. However, thanks to the courageous White defenders of Europe at Constantinople the Franks eastern flank and our race's living space in Europe were secured.

This battle fought at Constantinople from 717 to 718 AD kept the dark forces of Islam from overrunning Southeastern Europe, and possibly all of Europe! They were on a holy mission to mongrelize our race by bringing them under the yoke of their Semitic mud god. Our outnumbered White racial comrades in Constantinople were all that protected our Southeastern front at this time. The muds came with a horde of soldiers and the biggest fleet of ships that had been put together in the middle ages so far. However, their powerful assault on the city's walls was heroically repulsed by the White warriors manning them. Their amateurish attempt to blockade the city from other sea ports went up in flames when they were introduced to Greek fire. Then the shortsighted besiegers starved and froze to death through the winter. Their spring offensive and second attempt to starve the White men of Constantinople into slavery was turned into ashes, as well. It was all over after Leo III turned the Asiatic enemies of our race against the Arab enemies of our race, so the defeated Muslim retreated. This great victory secured our people's living space in Europe from Islam for centuries, and it is one of the many important stands made by the valiant warriors of our White race.

Tours 732

One of the most decisive battles in European history was fought at Tours in AD 732. The European Franks came together to defend their land from the Moorish Afro-Arabs who came to conquer Europe. Frankish infantrymen tried to defeat the Moorish cavalrymen as soon as they came over the Pyrenees Mountains, but the Franks were pushed aside by the overwhelming numbers of the invaders. The Franks quickly set up a new force of infantrymen directly in the path of the invaders at a place called Tours. The cavalrymen charged forward as soon as they saw the warriors of the West blocking their way, but the Franks held their ground. They attacked the Franks over and over again for days. However, the Franks could not be beaten and the Moors had no choice but to leave after they were defeated at Tours.

The Franks were a noble and strong Germanic people that once dwelled in the regions of the Rhine river. One group of Franks known as the Salians conquered Gaul around AD 500 and founded a great kingdom. It is because of these great people that Gaul later became the nation of France. At the time of the battle of Tours the Franks were lead by a brave and intelligent man named Charles Martel, also known as the Hammer, who had recently united the Austrasians and Neustrian Franks.

The Moors were a mongrel Afro-Arab people from the Middle East and North Africa who had conquered most of Spain by AD 713. They had been raiding in Southern France until Abd-er-Rahman, the Arabian emir of occupied Spain, led a huge invasion force across the Pyrenees Mountains with the intent to conquer and enslave Europeans.

A brave man named Duke Eudes (Odo) of Aquitaine led a group of Frankish infantrymen to try and stop the invasion of their homeland. This small group of Franks was no match for the 60 000 Afro-Arab cavalrymen that charged at them. Thus the brave Europeans were pushed aside...

Charles Martel quickly put together another force of Frankish infantrymen and positioned his warriors between Tours and Poitiers. He set them up in a solid square formation directly in the path of the invader. The Franks then hurriedly prepared themselves to defend their land and people.

When the Moors saw the Franks blocking their paths they charged into the European infantrymen. The Moorish cavalrymen slashed their swords down in the faces of the Frankish infantrymen and tried to push them aside with their overwhelming strength. This tactic usually gave the victory to the cavalrymen, the only way to stop the cavalry charge was to keep the square formation together and kill the cavalrymen, and that is just what the franks began to do!

The Moors charged at the Franks over and over again, but the Franks held their ground. They stabbed and chopped at the Afro-Arab cavalrymen with their swords and axes every time they attacked. The slaughter went on like this for at least four days. This was one of the few times in the Middle Ages when infantrymen stood their ground against cavalrymen. The Franks were supposed to break apart and run away from the Moors, but someone must have forgot to tell them. They refused to lose in this battle for their loved ones and land. They continued to kill the foreigners and the horses they rode in on. Even Abd-er-Rahman himself was cut down by the Europeans he had come to enslave.

Finally the foreigners began to lose their desire to die in these cavalry charges that were not going as planned. So the Moors had no choice but to retreat in the darkness of night. It was unnecessary for the European Franks to chase them, because the Mongrels were beaten men. The biggest thing that the invaders had to show for their attempted conquest was the large number of dead Moors that covered the fields at Tours.

In AD 732, the Europeans won a decisive victory in the battle of Tours. The Germanic Franks were united by Charles Martel and ready to fight the Moorish invaders. They courageously tried to stop the invasion of their kingdom as soon as the Moors crossed the Pyrenees Mountains, but the 60 000 Moorish cavalrymen overran their positions. However, the Franks set up a new position at Tours, and prepared for round 2 in their fight for their people's freedom. The foreigners charged at the

Europeans as soon as they saw them ready to defend their land, but the Franks held their ground. They were knocked back by the Frankish infantrymen every time they attacked and the battle raged for days. After losing many of their men, the Moors finally accepted defeat and they never tried to conquer the franks again.

Lechfeld 955 AD

The battle of Lechfeld in 955 AD put a stop to the Asiatic reign of terror in Europe. Our White race was up against an alliance of mud tribes who had already taken over large areas of our living space. The German states were united under one leader just in time to face this powerful force that wanted their land, and women next. Germany was invaded in 955 by a huge army of Asiatic horsemen. This forced the White knights of Germany to come and fight the Asian army that they knew was much bigger than their own. On August 9th they rose early and began their march toward the lopsided battle that awaited them. It began very badly for the Germans, and they should have lost. However, their leaders' will to fight kept them going. The king's bold words of encouragement drove his White warriors straight into the mud's teeth. This battle was then turned into a type of fight that the White men knew how to excel in. After ten hours of combat the Asians were broken. Over the next few days they were given everything that they had coming to them for the centuries of pain they had caused our people. This underdog victory literally changed the face of Europe, and it should never be forgotten.

About a hundred years after the Huns were driven out of Europe, their descendants launched a new invasion in 550 AD. Over the next few centuries hundreds of thousands of White people were killed for their land in eastern and central Europe. Our brave men would sometimes defeat a tribe of these Asiatics, but another tribe would always take its place. Then three of these mud peoples known as the Avers, the Khazars, and the Finno-Ugric joined forces to become the Magyars. They went on to occupy the area we call Hungary today, and in the 10th century they were launching raids from this area into Western Europe. None of our race's lands would be safe if this Asiatic invasion continued.

Our German brothers and sisters were hit hard by these raids. They had been a divided people since the breakup of Charlemagne's Empire. Then in 936 AD, many of the German princes chose a Saxon Duke named Otto as their king. He had grown up fighting his own people and the Magyars. So, he spent the next couple of decades bringing his Volk together. He believed that Germany could only be a country if it was one realm with one people and one leader. This is why he became "Otto I" and the king of the "first Reich". So, in 955 AD the newly unified White people of Germany were determined to keep trying to defend their race and nation.

The Magyars fought as light mounted bowmen, and they also carried slashing-type swords to use in close combat. They normally swept through the lands they raided, and they liked to pick our armies apart from a distance. A mud named Lel was in command of the Magyars when they came into Germany in 955. This "raid" was more like an invasion, though, because this time they stopped to put the Bavarian town of Augsburg under siege.

Otto I and 10,000 gallant White knights did the only honorable thing they could. They marched for Augsburg! As soon as the Magyars learned of the approaching Germans they withdrew from the city and made camp along the Lech River. When Otto I's men arrived in the area he had them make camp too, but they chose to make theirs upriver from the enemy's. It must have been very hard for any of the White men to eat or sleep knowing that the Asian army was so huge.

They rose early the next morning on August 9th, and put on their heavy armor. Then they formed up into a column of heavy cavalry and headed toward the enemy camp. Their column was made up of units of many German states. Three groups of Bavarians led the way, with Franconians, led by Conrad, behind them. The Saxons with Otto I were in the middle. Then the rear was brought up by Swabians and Bohemians. The column was moving over a rough path along the Lech River.

Then suddenly disaster struck! An unseen force of Asians stormed across the river and attacked the German flank! The Swabians and Bohemians were scattered by this surprise assault. The whole column was now caught between two large mud units, and it looked like it was all over. The White men were doomed!

Otto I refuse to face the facts, though, and he ordered Conrad's Franconians to re-secure the rear. They moved as fast as they could and overran the muds behind them. While this was going on Otto was already ordering the column to break up and form a battle line facing the muds coming at their front. No matter what, the White men were going to fight! So, Otto I kicked his spurs into his horse and led the charge!

As the red headed king led his White warriors forward he yelled these words to them: "They surpass us, I know, in numbers, but neither in weapons nor in courage. We know also that they are quite without the help of God, which is of the greatest comfort to us. Survival of the strong!!!" Then a hail of Magyar arrows slammed into them, but the charge continued. The muds were notching more arrows to their bows when the White knights and their wild-eyed war horses crashed into them!

They were hit with bone-crunching force by the heavy cavalrymen, and many of them lost their lives when they were struck down by the Germans' long swords. Lel then ordered his Magyars to fake a retreat in order to break up the White battle formation, but the mud's trick failed. The White knights stayed together, and kept coming at the Asians. They used their heavy armor as an equalizer against the muds' overwhelming numbers, and began to chop down their enemies in close combat. So, the battle was now being fought on the White man's terms.

It raged on and on like this for ten hours at

Lechfeld. Finally, the Asians could no longer take it, and they began to flee for their lives. The Germans were not done, though, so many muds continued to die. A lot of them drowned as they tried to make it across the Lech river. Others were cut to pieces on the river bank, but many were able to run off to hide in the countryside.

The years of murder and rape had caught up with these yellow dogs though, and most of these muds who ran off to hide were killed, too. A few lucky ones were allowed to live after having their noses and ears cut off. However, the vast majority of the 50,000 Magyars who had come to exterminate the White people of Germany were killed.

A lot of the ones who had stayed back in Hungary moved east after hearing of this blood bath. This is why there are only small traces of their Asiatic features seen in a minority of the people who live in Hungary today. Many Germanic and Slavic peoples moved there in the centuries that followed this victory. This is why the term "Magyar" is more of a cultural term for the people of Hungary. It is not a racial term like many try to persuade us to falsely believe, and our race should always be grateful to the valiant Germans who fought at Lechfeld for this fact!

This victory is very important, because it put an end to the genocide of our people in Europe that was being carried out by the eastern Asiatic peoples. It is one of the longest and worst hate crimes in world history, and the muds tried as hard as they could to complete it. We were saved, because the Germans came together just in time. The Magyar siege of Augsburg forced the Germans to make a hard decision. When they set out to defend their Fatherland, they knew that the odds were against them. On August 9th, they bravely marched toward their enemies. The battle started with the White men being attacked from behind. Otto I's steely resolution to fight back when all looked to be lost played a big part in this battle. He led by example and his powerful words filled his men with courage just when they needed it most. The White knights hit the muds with every ounce of flesh and iron that they had. After ten hours of fighting, the Asian will for battle was smashed. Not many of them made it out of Germany. This great event brought on a period of some much-needed ethnic cleansing in Europe that made Hungary and other nations in the area the predominantly White countries that they are today. Therefore, we should honor this victory by keeping them that way!

Constantinople 1453 AD

In 1453 AD an outnumbered band of White brothers made a hopeless stand against the Ottoman Army at Constantinople. The Ottoman Turks were a mongrelized people who had been foolishly allowed into Europe, and who then initiated a race war against the Whites who lived there. Constantinople was the only threat to their flank after they overran large areas of Southeastern Europe, so they decided to take this old symbol of white power with overwhelming force. In a couple of weeks the city was under attack and completely surrounded. However, the White warriors defending Constantinople were amazingly able to successfully fight back the numerous assaults that were launched at, under, and over the city's walls for months! They could not go on forever though, and this knowledge is what motivated the muds to make one more assault. While holding back their enemies in front of them the White heroes defending the city were stabbed from behind, but even as they stared into death's brown face they refused to surrender! This battle began a dark period in the history of our White race.

The Ottoman Turks were the successors of the Seljuk Turks and they got their name from the man who led this succession Osman. By the 14th century these mixed race muds were the leading military power of the Islamic religion, and they were determined to spread this mud faith into Europe by any means necessary. This is why it is shocking to learn that a Byzantine Emperor invited them into Europe! He hired them to fight against a rival to the Byzantine throne, but they decided to stay after the fighting was over.

They wasted no time, and captured the city of Gallipoli in 1354. Then they began pouring their troops into this beach head. The next thing that their leader Emir Orkhan did was to institute a tax of 1,000 babies from the defenseless White women in the area that had to be paid every year. These boys were then raised to serve as slave soldiers for the Ottoman Army, and they quickly became known as the elite corps of "Janissaries". With these brain polluted bastards they went on to defeat several White armies, and overran a lot of the Balkan Peninsula. They also got their hands on White designed cannons, and one of them was known as the "Basilica". It was 27 feet long and able to shoot stones as heavy as 600 pounds. By 1452 this powerful enemy force was armed and ready to eliminate the threat to its flank Constantinople.

The Byzantine Empire's capital city of Constantinople had stood as a bulwark against the mixed race invaders of the East for over a thousand years! It had never been the same though after being sacked by a White Christian army in the fourth crusade, and the majority of the city's population by 1452 was just as racially mixed as the Turks. It also had a Jewish community as well, and this city of tens of thousands only had an army of 7,000 White men to defend it. This small force was under the command of a well know Italian soldier named Giovanni Giustianini, and the city was ruled by the Byzantine Emperor Constantine XI. This city was not only a possible threat to the Ottoman' army's flank. Its location on the European side of the narrow sea that connects the Black sea to the Mediterranean sea also made it a very valuable naval prize as well...

So, on April 6th 1453 the Ottoman Sultan arrived at Constantinople to personally take charge of the army of a hundred thousand that came to take it. This army had an elite corps of White Janissaries as well as 70 White designed cannons including the Basilica. The majority of the land forces were placed on the Western land facing the side of the city, and the smaller portion was sent to capture the town of Pera that controlled the land on the opposite side of Constantinople's harbor known as the Golden Horn.

The cannons opened fire on the city, and created a breach in 12 days. This first breach was successfully defended by the White men though. Then a group of daring White sailors broke through the mud blockade and delivered some much needed supplies to the city. Mohammed then took advantage of his control of the strip of land on the other side of Constantinople's chain sealed harbor, and ordered his men to drag their ships over the land to place them in the harbor. This was a great feat of mud manual labor, and sadly the white counter attack that was meant to resecure the harbor was betrayed to the Turks by one of the many thousands of muds who lived in Constantinople. Therefore, the city was now under siege with no hope of getting any more food from Europe's ports, and the 7,000 White defenders would not get any reinforcements either.

Heavy stones then continued to hammer down on parts of the city's walls, and another breech was created on May 6th. Guistiniani immediately led his men to build a back up wall behind the opening and this feat of White combat engineering helped the defenders prevent the muds from making it into the city during the three hours of hard fighting against the Turkish assault. Another section of wall came down on the 12th, and the mud attack that came at it was only successfully thrown back by a last minute counterattack carried out by Constantine's Imperial Guard.

So far the outnumbered heroes defending Constantinople's walls were able to stop every assault that came at the breaches created by the Ottoman's army artillery. This forced Mohammed to order his men to begin mining tunnels under the city's walls in order to plant explosives under them, and bring down sections of wall not being properly guarded by the thinly spread defenders. However a White man named Johannes Grant personally led an ingenious countermining operation that found and destroyed all fourteen of the muds mining attempts.

After the failure of that idea Mohammed ordered his men to build a siege tower so that it could provide them with cover fire as they went over the city's walls. This siege tower was then rolled towards a part of Constantinople's wall that was unprotected, because its wall tower had been damaged by cannon fire. It then successfully covered the advance of a large body of Turks who then piled up against the city's wall, so they could go over it. this was such a critical situation that Emperor Constantine had to put out a call for volunteers to save this position, and as always many brave White men came forward. They then began to recklessly expose themselves. While they threw pots of an ancient form of napalm at the enemy siege tower, and others rebuilt the damaged wall tower at the same time! So, once again White valor had won the day!

Unfortunately, these starving, and exhausted heroes could not keep pulling off superhuman feats like this forever. This fact is what convinced Mohammed to try and take the city one more time. Most of his men wanted to retreat, but a small group of Turkish officers believed that a breakthrough could be made at the most damaged part of the city's wall where the Lycus River entered it.

This last try was launched late in the day of May 28th. The muds fired all their guns and then charged as soon as the wall came down. The White defenders fired every firearm, and arrow that they could at the oncoming wave of muds and held their ground. They were then attacked again though before they could even catch their breath! They held their ground against this attack too! They had been fighting for hours at this point, and they could barely stand up on their feet when they were immediately attacked again! This time they were hit by the White Janissaries!

While they were fighting to throw back this assault a gate on the wall north of their position was opened! A lot of survivors of this battled claim it was opened by a group of Jews. Anyways, a few Turks made it up to one of the city's near towers and raised their flag. This made the White men defending the breach believe that they had been flanked. Their gallant commander Guistiniani was also shot in his chest at this time! This tragic turn of events made the defenders pull back from the wall, and the whole mud army began pouring into the city. The battle was lost!

Emperor Constantine XI was urged by all the men around him to run while he still had the chance. He looked at one of them and said: "The city is taken and I shall still live?" Then he drew his weapon, and led a defiant charge into our race's enemies. The majority of the remaining White warriors died a hero's death with the last Emperor of the Byzantine Empire. All of the city's people except the Jews were enslaved by the victorious Turks.
The Muslim invaders of Europe no longer had to fear any possibility of a flank attack from the city of Constantinople. They also had control over one of the most important naval bases in Europe. The city was renamed Istanbul and made the capital city of the Ottoman Empire. Our White race was now in a fight to the death against a major land, and naval power!

This was the beginning of one of the darkest periods of our people's history, and whole nations of our race would get exterminated by the Ottoman Empire...

The 1453 battle of Constantinople was lost before it began, but the White men defending the city went down fighting anyway! All of the land around the city was already under mud occupation and they had plenty of their own White warriors as well as White technology to use against the old city. The defenders were quickly put under a tight siege, but they fought off every assault launched against the city for months! Time was not on their side though, and this fact fueled the muds as they carried out their final assault. The White heroes were betrayed while making their valiant last stand and this heinous act reminds us to never trust a mud! They lost this battle, but they never lost their courage! Our noble people would need heroic examples like this to inspire them in the dark times that came after this battle.

Granada 1491-92

There are only a few instances in the history of our race that can be compared to the comeback that was made by the White people of Spain at Granada. In order to fully comprehend the significance of this event one must first recognize the fact that the White people of Spain had been conquered, and then humiliated by foreigners for centuries! Their world was a hopeless place to live in until a red headed, blue eyed heroine came forward to become their savior. She and her valiant husband led the White people of Spain with an unflinching determination to take back what was theirs until they were able to choke their enemies into submission at Granada.

In 711 AD the Southwestern European land of Spain was invaded by a horde of Afro-Arab Mohammedan Moors who had crossed the narrow sea between Spain and North Africa. The Germanic Visigoths who ruled Spain at this time fought mostly as infantrymen, and they were outmaneuvered in every early battle that they engaged their enemies in. These mud horsemen were practically unbeatable out in the open, so the White defenders tried to fight them from behind the walls of their cities. However, the Jews, who had been allowed to live among the Spanish, betrayed them by opening the gates of many of these besieged cities to the invaders, so most of Spain was overrun in less than a year. Only a few areas in the north were spared from mongrel occupation after the Spanish won their first major victory at the battle of Covadonga in 718.

The so-called "free" Spanish kingdoms in the north were then forced to give the sandniggers a yearly payment of young White girls in exchange for peace! In the years that followed, the Moors invaded France too but they were miraculously defeated at tours by the Franks in 732. The Spanish had to keep paying the "White girl tax" until 791 when they were finally strong enough to stop this abomination from continuing! They even began to take back some of their land from the Moors, little by little, they fought as hard as they could as individual kingdoms, but the Jews that had betrayed them were still allowed to feed upon them. Therefore, Spain's humiliation continued…

In 1451, a fair princess named Isabella was born into this hopeless world where the south of her country was occupied by the Moors, her people were divided, and the Jews held some of the highest positions in Spain. Our noble race's enemies had no idea that this little White princess was their worst nightmare. She grew up around the filth that covered her kingdom, but she came through it all strong. After she married a gallant prince named Fernando from the kingdom of Aragon, she was crowned Queen Isabella of Castile and Lyon on December 12th 1474, the two most powerful kingdoms were now united and it was time to fight!

Isabella's first challenge as Queen was an invasion of her land by Portugal. She raised an army of her own to join forces with one from her husband's kingdom and this Spanish army defeated the Portuguese. Then on February 6th 1481 Queen Isabella instituted the Spanish Inquisition to smoke out the treasonous Jews who had been masquerading around as Christians. The Moors invaded her kingdom on Christmas day in 1482, and King Fernando quickly led the White men of Spain into a counterattack.! Queen Isabella served her people as the army's recruiting agent, the commissary, the head nurse, the propagandist and the purchaser of munitions. She even sold her personal jewelry to pay for the army's canons! The Spaniards fought fanatically for eight years with Isabella's zealous support, and in 1490 they chased the muds into the city of Granada.

The city of Granada had great fortresses as well as a wall around it with a thousand towers! Granada was put under siege and for the first months there was little fighting. Then in July 1491 the muds came out to engage their besiegers. During the combat a Moor named Yarfe threw a spear at King Fernando's pavilion before the Spanish beat the mongrels back into the city. This act infuriated the Spaniards, so they decided to sneak into Granada at night, and disrespect the Muslim muds by putting a copy of the Catholic Ave Maria prayer up on the door of a mosque!

Queen Isabella arrived shortly after the first

clash of the battle to pay her beloved soldados a visit at the front and she was protected by a bodyguard formation led by the Marquise of Cadiz Don Rodrigo Ponce de Leon. The Queen had requested a halt on operations because she did not want any of her men to put themselves in danger for her. However, the Queen's peace was violated when Yarfe, the spear chucker rode his horse out in front of the Spanish with the Ave Maria tied to its tail! A valiant White knight immediately requested to face Yarfe in single combat, and King Fernando quickly gave his consent.

The valiant Spaniard fought his opponent from horseback at first until they both went to the ground where they continued to swing steel at one another. Then after a close struggle that raged back and forth, the White man prevailed over the uppity sandnigger! The muds who had come out to watch the duel, had no respect for the White chivalry that honored the victory of a fair one on one fight, so they attacked the Spanish when Yarfe was killed. Granada's cannons fired on the Spaniards, but with the help of Isabella's bodyguards the White warriors cut down 2,000 of the mongrels before driving the rest of their enemies back into the city.

So far the battle was going well for the Spanish, but then a fire was accidentally started that practically burned their whole camp down! They persevered though and they even formed up to march in front of the city to prove that they were undefeated by this disaster. The muds then rushed out of Granada to attack them, but the White men whipped them again. After this last failure, the Moors spent the rest of the battle hiding behind their walls and starving. Finally on January 1ˢᵗ 1492 the Moorish King of Granada, Mohammed XI (Abu Abdullah Beabdil) came out and surrendered the keys to the city to King Fernando and Queen Isabella.

All of Europe celebrated with Spain on the day that the battle of Granada was won, because on this day an area of land was finally returned to our White race that had been held by the Islamic muds for almost 800 years! In Spain the violence continued though, because when the victors entered the city they found out that the king's prime minister as well as most of his top advisors were Jews! Queen Isabella was so angry with the Jews for their never ending support of her people's enemies that she expelled everyone of them that refused to convert to Christianity. Of course in hind sight we know she should have expelled the Jews as a race and not just as a religion. Nevertheless her action was better than no action at all, and for the rest of her reign her people were free from Muslim mud occupation as well as Jewish manipulation.

Not many people have ever been able to come back after being held down so low for so long like the White people of Spain were. They had been victimized by the muds and the Jews for hundreds of years! Yet in the end they proved the fact that if you stay White you can one day make things right! When I first read about Queen Isabella's courageous leadership in book II, chapter 12 of Nature's Eternal

Religion by Ben Klassen her story gave me hope for a victorious outcome in the bitter struggle that our race is in today. She yanked the Jews fangs out of her nation's neck just like Hitler did in post-WWI Germany, and then did everyting in her power to make the White people in Spain the masters of their own land. All of this is what makes Spain's triumph at Granada in 1492 one of the greatest achievements in world history!

Vienna 1529

The Ottoman Empire's seemingly unstoppable advance into Europe was violently halted by the defenders of Vienna in 1529. The Empire of mongrelized Muslims had already overrun large areas of southeastern Europe, and they were determined to deliver the death blow to our White race at Vienna. This great city was the main obstacle blocking the invader's path at that time, and White men came from as far away as Spain to come help defend it. The Ottoman army was huge, and there was little hope of stopping it. However, the soldiers at Vienna refused to run, and they did a miraculous job of getting the city ready for a fight. The Muds were shown nothing but defiance when they arrived at Vienna, so the invaders began mining operations in order to make holes in the city's walls to attack through, and it didn't take long for them to succeed. They ran into unexpected problems when they assaulted the breaches in Vienna's walls, though, and they were caught off guard by European counterattacks, as well. The battle then raged for weeks, and the city refused to be taken. Vienna's determination to resist destroyed the Ottoman army's will to continue the fight. The Turks were forced to retreat after failing to take the city. Our people's struggle for existence was far from over after this victory, but the Muds would never look at Vienna the same way again.

The Ottoman Empire was created by a band of

mongrelized horsemen known as Turks, and they were devout Muslims, too. They had been enslaving White people in southeastern Europe for hundreds of years, and they had stolen large areas of land by the 16th century. At that time, they were under the leadership of their ninth Sultan, named Suleiman, and in 1526 he led his army into Hungary. The city of Buda was captured, and a traitor named John Zapolya was placed on the throne to serve the Muds. As soon as Suleiman left, the Hungarians rebelled, because many of them wanted to have Archduke Ferdinand of Austria placed on their throne. This angered Suleiman, so he decided to come back with his army to crush White power in Europe once and for all!

Archduke Ferdinand was a member of the noble German Hapsburg family, and his seat of power was at Vienna in Austria. This city is located in central Europe, and it was the only thing keeping the Turks out of the western half of the continent. It could not be allowed to fall, so Ferdinand sent out for help. The Holy Roman Emperor, Charles V, heard him, and Spanish as well as German soldiers answered the call to arms. They were some of the finest soldiers of Europe, and they brought Vienna's garrison from 16,000 to 24,000. This force was small, but it would have to hold if the White race was going to survive.

The Ottoman army was 250,000 strong, though, and a lot of its soldiers were just as good as any White man. In fact, many of them *were* White men, because the Muds had been ripping White babies from their crying mother's arms for hundreds of years. These boys were then raised to become slave soldiers, and they were the elite of the Ottoman army known as Janissaries. This giant force began its march on April 10, and it went first into Hungary to slaughter the White freedom fighters who had dared to fight slavery. To make matters worse, there were also 20,000 Muds on horseback pillaging the countryside. So, the future of the White race was looking very dark.

While the Ottoman army marched, the defenders of Vienna were working miracles. The 250-year-old walls of the city were in serious need of repair, and there was not going to be enough time to fix them properly, but in a remarkable display of leadership a man named Graf Nicholas zu Salm-Reifferscheidt stepped up to become the de facto commander. He had the houses closest to the wall dismantled to create a clear field of fire for the 72 canons that he personally oversaw the placement of, and then he had the debris from the houses used to repair the city's walls as best as possible. All of this work was an amazing demonstration of White resourcefulness by Graf Nicholas and the people of Vienna.

On September 23, a force of Turkish cavalry arrived at the city, but a gallant group of White knights rode out to skirmish with them as soon as they were seen. The Ottoman army had grown to 350,000 by now, and it had Vienna surrounded by the 27th. Suleiman sent four White prisoners into the city with his surrender demands, but Graf Nicholas and his men refused even to dignify Suleiman with a response. Instead, four Turkish prisoners were sent to Suleiman with no answer.

The Muds then began mining operations so they could blow breaches in the city's walls by placing explosives under them. They had to do this, because they had failed to prepare for the unexpectedly wet weather that stopped their heavy siege guns, as well as their feed wagons, from keeping pace with the main army. The defenders began counter-mining operations, and they did have some early successes. It did not take the Turks long though, before they were able to bring a section of the wall down. The gap that was created was big enough for even cavalry to charge through, so the Ottoman army rushed forward to take Vienna.

As soon as the Muds and their slave soldiers came at the breach, though, they found stout-hearted White men waiting for them. With clenched teeth, the defenders of Europe gripped their weapons and drove them straight into the invaders' guts! This bitter resistance sent the attackers right back the way they had come. Then the Turks continued to create more breaches. While they worked, they themselves were attacked by swarms of White daredevils who launched hit-and-run raids in and out of the Ottoman army's positions.!These heroes would then return back into the city.

The Muds also had 300 canons that they fired at the city throughout the fighting, but the city's

White gunners continued dutifully to man their 72 guns in the face of this overwhelming fire. It went on and on like this as the days turned into weeks. More gaps were opened in the walls, but the valiant White men defending the city never gave up! They were Vienna's backup walls! These courageous soldiers took terrible wounds while holding back the waves of attackers, but they manfully remained on their feet to keep fighting for their blood, soil, and honor! They killed 1,200 elite Janissaries in one of the engagements alone!

These bloody defeats broke the will of the Ottoman army. Even Suleiman could see that the battle was not going the way it was supposed to go. For the first time in the Janissaries' 200 year history, they began to complain in this battle that they were being wasted in the failed attempts to take Vienna. Suleiman was desperate to win the battle before his army could run out of food, so he bribed his White soldiers to make one more attack.

On October 14, 1529, another section of Vienna's wall came down, and the Janissaries rushed forward once again, though they ran into cursing, wild-eyed White men slamming sharp pikes into them, and death! After this last attempt failed, the Muds gave up, and the tents that covered the ground as far as the eye could see were taken down. They burned their White prisoners alive, too, before beginning their retreat. European cavalrymen followed them and painted the fresh snow red with the blood of the Ottoman soldiers they cut down.

They lost many of their men to these vengeful White knights who turned their retreat into a cold, slow death march.

This great victory destroyed the false belief in the Ottoman Empire's invincibility. Europe's struggle against the Turks was far from over, and they would come back to Vienna. However, this battle turned Vienna into a city that would represent the White race's defiance against the mongrelized Muslims of the East, because in this battle a handful of brave Europeans let the Muds know that they had only begun to fight!

The White warriors that refused to be enslaved by the Ottoman Empire at Vienna in 1529 won a huge victory for our race. The Muds had every intention of crashing into Western Europe and mongrelizing our people. The heroes at Vienna kept this from happening. The Turks had all the advantages and it looked like there was no way they could lose this battle. A small force of Europeans believed otherwise though, and they got Vienna ready for a fight anyway. Their brazen behavior toward the overwhelming might of the Turk set the tone for the fighting that followed. The Turks dug their mines and brought down parts of the city's walls. This didn't do much for them in the end though, because the defenders proved that walls don't protect a city, men protect a city! White men protected their race at Vienna! On October 14, the Muds retreated and many of them were hunted down like dogs while they marched. This great victory renewed our people's faith in their arms and it turned Vienna into a bastion of White power that would continue to hold back the Turks for centuries to come.

Lepanto 1571

In 1571 the divided Europeans who lived in the Mediterranean area did what was best for the White race by joining forces to fight their common racial enemies in the battle of Lepanto. Their very existence was threatened by a powerful non-White empire. The relentless aggression of this non-White empire towards the Europeans is what convinced them to set aside the frivolous issues that they had between one another and form a White alliance. Those who controlled the Mediterranean sea exercised a large amount of power over its coastal countries, so our people's struggle for survival was going to be decided in this area on the water. So, the White men of Europe set sail to take the fight to the muds, and the clash that followed when these two sides made contact effected the entire region.

The powerful mixed race Ottoman Turkish Empire already occupied large areas of our White race's living space in Southeastern Europe by the middle of the 16th century, and its navy was working side by side with the North African Berber Pirate states against our people living in the Mediterranean. In Spain there was already a big population of Moriscos (Moorish Christian converts) who were ready and willing to secure a beachhead for their mud brothers to invade Spain from. So, the Turks and Berbers encouraged the Moriscos to rise up against the Spaniards.

Philip II, the King of Spain, was sadly caught off guard when the muds in his country turned on his real countrymen, because he was busy fighting other white Christians over whose interpretation of Christianity was better. Once he learned that the Christian muds in his country had joined forces with the Islamic muds though, he sent his young half brother Don Juan of Austria to crush them in 1568. This did not stop the Turks from looking for other pieces of Europe to conquer though.

In 1570, the Ottoman navy landed an army on the Venetian held island of Cyprus, and the Venetians quickly appealed to any other Europeans that would help them. This latest mud act of aggression against a lone European country was just what was needed to get the White men to wake up! Pope Pius V, King Philip and the North Italian State of Genoa immediately formed an alliance called the Holy League. Then they assembled a fleet of 208 galleys, 6 galleasses and about 100 large cannon carrying ships with their Venetian partners at the Port of Messina on the island of Sicily. However, as they were preparing to relieve Cyprus's defenders, they got news that the island had fallen to the Turks and that the defenders had all been either murdered or enslaved.

With no hope of saving their brothers on Cyprus the eighty thousand White men got on their ships to find and engage the Ottoman Empire at sea. The White fleet was led by 26 year old Don Juan of Austria who had smashed the muds in Spain. On

October 7ᵗʰ 1571 they spotted the mud navy near the Turkish occupied island of Lepanto so they broke up their fleet into four formations to prepare for battle! A Venetian named Augustino Barbarigo commanded the northern left flank position in the shallow water near Cape Seraphia. Don Juan commended the heavy gun ships in the center, a well known Genoese admiral named Giovanni Andrea Beria commanded the southern right flank, and a reserve force was placed in the rear under the Marquis of Sante Cruz's command. A string of galleasses was sent forward as skirmishers.

The mud fleet was led by Ali Pasha and it was formed up similar to the European fleet, a Turk name Mahomet Sirocco held the northern right flank, the southern left flank was held by Berbers under Uluck Ali's command, and Ali Pasha commanded the center, all of their ships had White slaves chained to their oars, and Ali Pasha promised them freedom if they rowed his 85,000 man force to victory.

Don Juan sailed along in front of his fellow white warriors and shouted words of encouragement to them which they responded to with loud war cries! Then the skirmisher ships opened fire! Most of their shots as well as the shots that began coming from Don Juan's formation were strategically aimed at Ali Pasha's center position, and his ships were prevented from moving forward by this heavy fire. However, both of the mud flank formations kept advancing, so the 245 ships of the mud fleet quickly became separated from each other.

Sirocco's formation surprised the Europeans by sailing around them through shallower water closer to the shore of Cape Scrophia where they thought no one could go without bottoming out their ships. This allowed the muds to attack the Venetians from the side and Barbarigo was forced to fight to the death when they overwhelmed his flagship. Then, the muds got surprised when the new leaderless White men regrouped and counterattacked! Barbarigo's ship was recaptured, lost, and then recaptured again! Sirroco's advance was then halted after his own ship was destroyed, and was dragged from the wreckage by the White men from northern Italy like a wet rat.

Doria's position was also out flanked by Uluck Ali in the south. The Genoese and papal ships then made the mistake of turning their backs to Don Juan's position to fight Uluck Ali. This allowed Uluck Ali to make a move to exploit this unprotected gap between the European formations. However, the Marquis of Santa Cruz came in with his reserves, and stopped this sandnigger breakthrough dead in the water!

Throughout the battle, Don Juan's gunners threw everything they had at Ali Pasha's center formation, and as the Europeans advanced they opened up with their matchlock firearms! As soon as they got close enough, the brave soldados of Spain began lunging themselves aboard their enemies ships. Thus the battle became a bloody close quarters affair! The Europeans fought their way onto ship after ship, but it took them three costly attempts to make their way onto Ali Pasha's flagship. Once they were aboard Ali Pasha backed into a corner where he began to beg for his sorry life, but a battle crazed White man put an end to this pathetic sight by chopping the mud's head off. A European pikeman then forced Ali Pasha's head onto the end of his long weapon and raised it up high for all to see! This act put so much fear into the rest of the muds that the majority of them surrendered.

The battle of Lepanto ended with a lot of people dead on both sides, but the heroic sacrifices made by the White men of Europe were not made in vain. They killed over 30,000 muds, took 8,000 prisoners, and freed about 15,000 White men from slavery! The muds also lost 230 ships and the Europeans only lost 13! This victory cost the Europeans close to 15,000 casualties, but White people all over the continent cheered the news of this battle's outcome, sadly the White racial unity that made this victory possible did not last long, but the ripples that were caused by this explosion of White power on the Mediterranean sea traveled far into the region's future. In 1609, the next king of Spain Philip III kicked 250,000 of the Moriscos out of our race's living space, and in 1805 the Berbers of North Africa were blockaded into submission by the United States navy! Of course, neither of these things would have taken place if our people had not sunk the flower of the Ottoman Empire's navy to the bottom of the Mediterranean sea!

The battle of Lepanto is a glorious event in which White men of many nationalities ignored the petty differences that divided them, and instinctively did the right thing by teaming up to fight their real enemies. Their political and religious differences back then were more of a weakness than a strength. Fortunately for us, on October 7th 1571, they didn't do what was necessarily best for their own individual kingdoms, republics or Christian sects. No, on this day they fought together and they died together as White men! Today we have hordes of sandniggers coming over the Mediterranean sea to invade Europe again. We stopped them at the battle of Lepanto and if we come together again as one White race we will blow them out of the water like we did their ancestors.

Vienna 1683

One of Europe's most important battles was fought at Vienna in 1683. Vienna is the capital of Austria, and it was the home of the Hapsburg dynasty. The Ottoman Empire wanted to destroy Vienna because it was the main obstacle blocking them from conquering all of Europe. The Turks arrived at the city on July 17th and they quickly put it under siege before launching their assault against the city's wall. The Turks failed to make it over the walls so they began to mine their way under them. But on September 12th an army of 20,000 Europeans led by the King of Poland arrived and routed the invaders. Many more battles were fought between the Europeans and the Asiatic Turks. But the Ottoman Empire was never able to conquer all of Europe because it was stopped at the Gates of Vienna.

Vienna is the capital of the Central European nation of Austria. The Hapsburg dynasty gained control of Austria under the leadership of Albert V. He became the King of Hungary in 1438 and the Emperor of the Holy Roman Empire as Albert II the same year. Vienna stood as a bulwark against the Ottoman Empire's conquest of Europe over the next few hundred years. However, in 1683 the struggle against the Turks was far from over.

Turkey was the home of the Ottoman Empire, and it began as one of the three tribes of the Muslim Seljak Empire. The Ottoman Empire was founded by Osman I, and by 1354 it gained control of the European Gallipoli Peninsula. In 1365 it captured the European city of Adrianopole and made it the capital of the Empire. The Serbs, Bosnians and Albanians of South East Europe bravely defended themselves. But the Turks were too strong for them to stop. Many Europeans were killed or enslaved by the Turks as the army of the Ottoman Empire conquered one nation after another. The Turks were stopped from taking Vienna in 1529, but by 1683 they were ready for another try.

At this time the Ottoman Empire was ruled by the Sultan Mohammed IV, and he is the man who sent the Grand Vizer Kara Mustafa to destroy Vienna. The Turks reach the city on July 17th. Austria's Hapsburg Emperor Leopold I left the city, but the noble Count Ernst Rudiger von Starhemberg took control of Vienna's defence. Mustafa put the city under siege and then sent his men forward to assault the walls. The defenders of Vienna tenaciously fought off every assault wave that crashed into them. They persevered through artillery fire week after week. When one man died doing his duty on the wall another heroically took his place. The battle for Vienna raged for ever a month like this, but Vienna's walls, gates, and the valiant men defending them were unbreakable.

So Mustafa and his men had no choice other than to begin mining operations. This would allow them to go under the walls of Vienna. They could then overwhelm the Europeans and destroy them.

Thus, the fate of Western civilization was sealed. The defenders of Vienna knew they could not stop the Turks. Nevertheless the Europeans courageously refused to surrender. Instead of giving up, they loaded their muskets, sharpened their blades, and prepared to make their final stand. One European soldier even scratched a final statement on the wall that can still be read today. "Mustafa you dog go to hell!"

But before the Turks finished their mining operations something amazing happened. An army of 20,000 European warriors led by the King of Poland John III Sobieski arrived at the city. The order to charge was given, and the European cavalry and infantry stormed forward. They smashed through the Turkish siege lines, and began to shoot, stab and slash the invaders to pieces. The Asiatics who came to enslave Europe were routed.

The Ottoman Empire never tried to take Vienna again. Many more battles were fought over the next couple hundred years as the European nationalist revolutions liberated most of the Turkish occupied lands in Europe. By the early 20th century they were driven back to the Gallipoli Peninsula. They still hold some land in Europe today, but if the Turks were not stopped at Vienna in 1683 they would probably hold a lot more.

The victory that was won at Vienna in 1683 is one of the most important in European history, because it saved Europe. Vienna was the home of the

Hapsburgs, and the bulwark of Western civilization. The Ottoman Empire was the power house of Eastern civilization and its goal was the destruction of the West and the enslavement of its people. From July 17th to September 12th the Turks assaulted Vienna with everything they had, but the brave European defenders of the city held firm through it all. The Turks began to mine their way under the walls of the city, and it looked like they were going to win. But the King of Poland and 20,000 valiant Europeans came to the rescue and routed the army of the Ottoman Empire. The struggle against the Turks was far from over. But the Asiatic Ottoman Empire's dream of enslaving all of Europe ended violently at the gates of Vienna in 1683!

San Jacinto 1836

The victorious battle of San Jacinto brought an end to the brutal race war in Texas, and it also set into motion a chain of events that brought unimaginable prosperity to our White race. In the early 19th century our people were following their natural born urge to expand their living space, but the idle people of Mexico wanted us to stagnate alongside them instead. When they saw that they could not get us to lower ourselves to their level they tried to disarm us, but we quickly chased them out of Texas. The Mexicans returned with an army of thousands and they began to exterminate as many of our people as they could. Then a great man named Sam Houston rallied our White warriors to his banner, and then he cunningly baited the Mexican commander, General Santa Anna, into meeting us on the plain of San Jacinto for a fight on our terms. They got their noses bloodied as soon as they attacked, so they decided to pull back in order to wait for some help. The next day we lined up for battle after sending a small group to destroy the Mexicans' only escape route. General Houston then led the men onward and the Mexicans were attacked with so much fury that the battle ended violently in only 18 minutes. We made the half breeds pay dearly for every one of our people that they had murdered, and the killing continued for hours. They were so utterly defeated that Santa Anna had only one way to save his sorry ass, and that is why he gave up Texas. This victory paved the way for our noble race to also inhabit the rest of the land west of Texas, as well, and it is also a heroic event in our history that can still inspire our race today in our struggle.

By the early 19ᵗʰ century our great White race had been fighting its way westward for hundreds of years on the North American continent, because back then we still knew that we had been ordained by our creator to do so. At this time the land west of our temporary border was the mostly uninhabited northern Mexican state of Texas, and the idle half breeds living there had the audacity to invite us to become Mexican citizens in Texas in order to grow fat from the taxes they could later collect from our industriousness. Our people who settled in Texas soon grew tired of being servants for the Mexicans. I believe that a young white man living under Mexican rule in Texas named Noah Smithwich described the feelings of our people there best when he said, "It is not in the nature of things for the superior race to remain long under the domination of the inferior."

The Mexicans saw the writing on the wall, so in September of 1835 they tried to disarm the White people living in Gonzales, Texas, but they were chased off by a small group of brave White men and this incident kicked off a White revolution in Texas. Hundreds of White men from America armed with anything that could shoot lead and Bowie knives for backup came to help their kin fight with no support from the U.S. government. This barely-trained militia quickly whipped the professional soldiers of Mexico at the Battle of Concepcion on

October 28th, and then they ran the rest of the Mexican army out of San Antonio, Texas by December 9th.

President Santa Anna led an army of 6,000 Mexican soldiers with the intent of exterminating the White people living in Texas in 1836, and he surrounded about 150 White men in a mission called the Alamo in San Antonio on February 23rd. Among those men were legendary warriors like Davy Crockett, Jim Bowie, and William B. Travis. It was clear that everyone in the Alamo was going to die, but 30 selfless men and boys from the "Gonzales Ranging Company of Mounted Volunteers" snuck into the mission anyway to die with their brothers. However, one person lost his nerve, and that was a Jew named Louis Moses Rose, who slithered out of the Alamo like a coward on the last night of the siege. The final assault came on March 6th, and the Alamo's defenders died bravely after killing 1,600 Mexicans. Then disaster struck when 400 White men commanded by Col. Fannin of Goliad were caught in the open and defeated by a large force of Mexicans. They decided to surrender, because they didn't want to leave their wounded behind. The muds then murdered almost every one of them except for a few who made a run for it. When the news of these events reached the White settlements in eastern Texas, the women courageously began to move the defenseless White children toward the United States border, and the men became fighting mad with anger.

There was only one man in Texas at this

time who knew what needed to be done, and this great hero of our race was General Sam Houston. He knew that our barely-trained White militiamen could not beat the whole half breed horde at once or hold them off in a siege battle, so he decided to bait the bloodthirsty muds into recklessly pursuing us with a force closer to our size. He did this by dragging his angry men away from the Mexican army for as long as it took, and Santa Anna took the bait by chasing after Houston with only 850 hand-picked men. As soon as General Houston heard of this, he rallied our men to practically claw their way through 55 miles of muddy roads and cross bayous by raft, bridges, and even swimming in only two and a half days in order to place themselves in the path of the arrogant Mexicans. Then they waited in the woods on the edge of a plain at sea level called San Jacinto...

Santa Anna had big plans to trap our men at San Jacinto, because it was basically a kill zone surrounded by bodies of water, swampland, and marshes. There were only two ways of crossing over the plain, one of which was Lynch's Ferry. Santa Anna brought his soldiers onto the plain using the other way, Vince's bridge, and he was soon shocked to find out that he was the one who was trapped. He sent his men forward to attack our White men blocking Lynch's Ferry, and an artillery duel began. Our brave gunners gave the muds a bloody nose and knocked over their heavy canon. Then the half breeds lost their taste for battle and retreated three quarters of a mile in order to put their backs to a body of water called Peggy's Lake. Santa Anna didn't want to fight anything close to a fair fight anymore, so he ordered his soldiers to build a breastwork in front of their camp. Then the Mexicans waited for the reinforcements that they knew were close to catching up to them.

Four hundred more Mexicans arrived the following morning on April 21ˢ, but Santa Anna decided to stay behind his breastwork. General Houston, on the other hand, decided that it was now or never, so he sent a small group of men led by one of his best scouts known as Deaf Smith to destroy Vince's Bridge. There were going to be no more reinforcements or any chance of running away for anybody. Houston then formed up his men into two lines of infantry almost a thousand yards long with a cavalry force on the right flank and two canons (the twin sisters) in the center.

At four PM, General Houston led over 750 barely-trained White militiamen toward the 1,250 professional soldiers of the Mexican army. Soon after they began to march, Deaf Smith came riding up, yelling to the men that the bridge was down and everyone now knew that this battle was going to be a fight to the death. When they were 200 yards away from the Mexican line, the twin sisters opened fire. Then our White warriors charged forward with their muskets blazing. At this point, the muds heard three words they would never forget. "Remember the Alamo!" became a furious war cry yelled by hundreds of our men, and seven survivors of the Goliad massacre gave them two more words that froze the blood when they yelled, "Remember Goliad!" The breastwork was blown away, and a man named Jimmy Curtice, who had lost his son in law at the Alamo, began smashing in Mexican skulls using his gun as a club as he screamed like a berserker, "Alamo, you killed Wash Cottle!" The half breeds tried to fight back. They shot two horses out from under General Houston, as well as a few of our men, but they could not stop the White Power that had been unleashed upon them. Every mud that didn't run was shot, clubbed, or stabbed to death in 18 minutes.

The rest of the Mexicans started trying to surrender at this point, because they knew they had been defeated. The killing had just begun though, and the half breeds had nowhere to run. It was now time to pay for all the White men they had murdered. One of Houston's captains was heard yelling "Boys, you know how to take prisoners, take them with the butt of your guns, club guns, and remember the Alamo, remember Labaher (La Bahia or Goliad) and club guns right and left and knock their goddamn brains out!" Peggys's lake soon started to fill with bodies, and our white knights on horseback cut down any Mexicans who tried to run across the open plain. Only when it grew dark did we finally take anyone alive. A total of nine White men were killed or wounded, and 600 dead Mexicans were left on the field to feed the birds and wolves.

Santa Anna was last seen riding away for his life, but the next morning he was captured. Most of our men started looking for the nearest hanging tree, but General Houston offered Santa Anna his life in exchange for Texas. He cowardly took this deal, and ordered the rest of the Mexican army to retreat from Texas. At this time Texas had its own government, so a treaty was signed by Santa Anna that recognized Texas's independence. Santa Anna later went back on the deal he had made, and taught us never to trust the word of a non-White. However, he never tried to invade Texas again, because he and everyone else knew that it was now the land of the White man!

This victory also affected many White people all over the world, because it motivated the United States as well as many other governments to recognize Texas as a nation that could hold its own. This led Texas to later becoming a state of the American Union, and this started the US versus Mexico war. The half breeds were defeated in this war, and our people gained all the land west of Texas as well. Many White people from all over the world settled in this land and we still hold it today, it has brought us unimagined prosperity, and it has nourished generations of our race. These are the reasons that I believe San Jacinto is one of the greatest victorious battles in our race's history.

The victorious battle of San Jacinto put a stop to the extermination of our White race in Texas, and it also helped us extend the borders of our living space on the North American continent from sea to shining sea. The natural instincts that our people were following in the 19th century were good for them, because they kept our people from allowing themselves to become Mexican servants. At Gonzales, Texas, in 1835 our men refused to give up their right to bear arms, and then our people started a White revolution that chased the Mexican soldiers out of Texas. When the half breed horde came back in February of 1836 about 180 White men died violently after refusing to surrender at the Alamo, and their heroism as well as the atrocity committed against our POWs at Goliad made the blood in every White man's veins boil. General Houston's leadership ability is what made it possible to rally our vengeful men together, and catch the seemingly undefeated Mexican army off guard at San Jacinto. The violent reception that the half breeds got when they attacked was so unexpected that they fell back in shock from it, and built a breastwork to wait for reinforcements. On April 21st our men destroyed the Mexican's only way of escape, and lined up for a fight to the death. The muds then learned the true meaning of White Power, and they were smashed in 18 minutes. Then they also received some good old fashion White justice for the crimes they had committed against our race. This bloody defeat brought Santa Anna to his knees, and he quickly recognized the independent nation of Texas. The victory at San Jacinto also put our race on a path to a glorious expansions of our homeland that we could only have dreamed of, and I believe that the battle of San Jacinto can still inspire our great White race today in our fight for our blood, soil and honor!

Blood River 1838

Blood River was a climactic battle in one of the most epic adventures that members of our White race have ever set out on. In the 15ᵗʰ century many new lands were discovered by White explorers, and brave little groups of our people later brazenly went forth to places like South Africa to settle them. Life was hard in these new lands though, because the groups of White peoples had to contend with each other as well as hordes of colored savages that lurked behind every bush. The hardships that the White settlers endured at the hands of these savages in 1838 were too much for most men to take. Nevertheless, the naturally ordained bonds of marriages, family and race kept them in the fight. Then after months of struggle they made a river run red with the blood of their enemies in a battle that would help define their future nation's character.

The first White man to discover the Southern tip of Africa was a daring Portuguese explorer named Bartholomew Diaz, and the King of Portugal named this new land the "Cape of good hope." More than a century and a half later the first major White settlement was founded at the Cape in 1652 by Germanic Dutch peoples from Northwestern Europe. Later, in the early 19ᵗʰ century the Cape Colony was occupied by the ever expanding British Empire, and many of the laws introduced by the British were not liked by the Dutch farmers (Boers) who decided to move further inland.

The Boers were a lot like the American "Pioneers" of the wild west, and the savage tribes they faced in Africa were just as backwards as the savage tribes in America. One of the most dangerous paths to travel (Trek) inland was over the "Drakensberg" (the Dragon Mountains). In fact about 80% of the first two Trekker expeditions that attempted to make it over the Drakensberg were killed by savage blacks and malaria outbreaks. However, a third Trekker expedition led by a man named Piet Retief finally made it over the Drakensberg in 1838, and the jovial Boers quickly dubbed the land they saw before them as "Blydevooruitzicht" (Happy prospects).

On February 5th 1838 a black Zulu chief named Dingcan put his mark on a contract that granted Retief's Trekkers the land of modern day Kwa-Zulu-Natal in exchange for the Boers retrieving a herd of cattle that had been stolen from him. Then, the next morning on February 6th, Retief and his 70 man "commando" (mounted company) were asked to come inside Dingcan's large hut for a farewell toast. They left their guns outside to show the Zulus respect, so they had no chance when Dingcan ordered 2,000 of his best warriors to "kill the White wizards!" Retief's heart was carved out his chest, after he was forced to watch his son and all of his men killed…

On February 16th the rest of the Trekkers were still happily awaiting the return of Retief's commando after learning that he had secured land for them. So at 1:00 in the morning they were caught off guard when they were pounced on by 10,000 blood thirsty niggers! Some of the White women were stabbed to death with spears over 20 times! Others had their breasts hacked off of their bodies while they were still alive! A total of 41 men, 56 women and 185 little defenseless White children were murdered before the Boers were able to circle their covered wagons to defend themselves. When the sun finally came up the only word that the Boers could use to describe the aftermath of this atrocity was "Weenen" (Weeping). The niggers also attacked the British settlers at the Port of Natal, and they were just barely fought off by stiff White resistance.

All of the men still standing in what was left of Retief's expedition immediately decided to retreat now that half of their people had been killed, but the Boer women had other ideas. They righteously believed that the blood of their loved ones had to be avenged, and when words failed to convince the men to stay the wild eyed White women declared their intention to fight the niggers themselves! Sadly things went from bad to worse though, when, with the zealous support of their women, the men set out to fight the Zulus only to get caught in a nigger ambush…

When word of Relief's expedition's plight reached the White settlements hundreds of Boers, and three valiant Scotsmen, who had fought the nigger attack on the Port of Natal, volunteered to go to the survivors' aid! These hard northwestern European

White men were formed into a commando of 451 men with two small cannons under the command of a man named Andries Pretorius. Then they set out into the bush to take the fight to the niggers!

Pretorius led his commando through six days of running battles with the Zulus, before he found a good place to fight them in a decisive engagement next to the Neome River. He ordered the wagons to be formed into a triangle with one side running along the river bank, another side running along a deep ditch (dongo), and its longest side facing open ground. The Boers then gathered up huge amounts of thorn bushes, and stuffed them under the wagons facing open ground and filled up the dongo as well. Lanterns were also hung up on the outside of the wagons to help spot any night time nigger attacks. The Boers even promised to praise the Christ God every year on the battle's anniversary if he granted them victory.

On the morning of December 16th 1838 tens of thousands of spear chucking black savage Zulus advanced on the 451 White men. Pretorius coolly ordered the Boers and Brits to let their enemies get really close. Then, when the niggers were only about ten steps away, the White men opened fire! Large numbers of Blacks were hit, but they continued to come at the White men in screaming human wave assaults!

The niggers tried to attack across the river too, so the defenders brought one of their cannons into action. They assaulted this side of the wagons so ferociously that the cannon's gunners ran out of cannonballs. However, the ingenious White men had collected cannonball shaped stones to use as emergency ammunition, so no nigger ever made it across the river alive. In fact, the commando kept up such a fast rate of fire that the blacks were only able to get close enough to hit Pretorius and another White man with their spears.

At the very moment that Pretorius noticed the Black tide recede a little he ordered one of the wagons to be pushed aside to allow 150 mounted men to charge out towards the Zulus! The niggers were stunned by the unexpected sight of the White wizards advancing on them. An entire formation of 2,000 Zulus was smashed to pieces when the White men crashed into it, and commenced to kill! Many of the now panicked niggers then tried to escape the White knights by crossing to the other side of the river only to get hammered by musket and cannon fire. The water began to turn red with the blood of the dying savages, and this sight is what gave the battle of Blood River its name. There is no telling how many died after their bodies floated down the river or how many died later of their wounds after they ran away. What is known is that there were about 3,000 dead niggers left lying on the ground by sundown…

The battle of Blood River is an important event in South African as well as White history. The Boers and Brits fought the blacks until they submitted to White rule. They fought each other too, but battles like Blood River instilled a belief in the righteousness of their common struggle to tame the wild land they lived together on. They later built a nation together that performed the world's first successful heart transplant, built an industrial plant that turned coal into oil, and built its own nuclear weapons! However, battles like Blood River gave the Boers, Brits and White peoples all over the world the idea that their superiority over the non-White peoples obligated them to civilize the poor savages. They believed that the Christ god granted them victory at Blood River, and helping their enemies afterwards was the Christian thing to do. Today the Whites in South Africa live under nigger rule...

The battle of Blood River definitely ranks high among the victories achieved by our noble people in their courageous struggle to defend, and attain living space for our White race. The non-White invasions of Europe had made our people well drilled in the art of war when the age of discovery began. We quite literally came to lands like those in the south of Africa, saw them, and then conquered them. Many of our people lost their lives while making places like South Africa the land of the White man, but the eternal Laws of nature demand sacrifices to be made for rewards. No one gave us any of the lands we had in the past nor any of the lands we hold today. They were paid for in full with the blood of the Boer Trekkers, the American Pioneers of the West, the hardy Australians, the formidable Canadians, and many other brave descendants of the battle scarred defenders of Europe! Therefore, let us praise the victories like Blood River by protecting our White race's gene pool that contains the genetic qualities that gave us the ability to create our civilizations that produced the weapons that won us the lands we were destined by nature to rule!

Europeans at war

In Mother Nature's war for survival our European peoples have had some very hard times. Our very existence, as a matter of fact, has come close to being destroyed. Our enemies have taken control of our schools and media. We don't hear a lot about the struggles of our peoples as much as we hear about all the so called "crimes" we have committed against other peoples. Our enemies are slowly killing us with "White guilt". We need to teach our peoples about the struggles we have gone through so they will understand that they have nothing to feel guilty for.

In 490 BC, the Persians led an army of Eastern Asiatic peoples to enslave Greece and the rest of our European homeland. The Greek warriors from the city of Athens defeated the enemy at the battle of Marathon. The enemy came back in 480 BC with an army of 1 700 000. The Greek Spartans led a group of warriors to make a stand at Thermopyle against the enemy. The Spartans and their king Leonidas earned immortality in this battle when they fought to the death. The heroic example of sacrifice the Spartans gave at Thermopyle inspired the rest of the Greeks to fight and defeat the enemy.

The Semitic Phoenicians tried to enslave Europe as well. Rome fought three wars against these people whom they called Punic. In the second Punic war the enemy's greatest general Hannibal brought an army over the Alps in to Italy. In the Battle of

Cannae in 216 BC, his army killed and defeated thousands of Romans. The Roman commander Varro did not give up and made an effort to carry on the struggle. On his return to Rome he was publicly thanked by the citizens because no matter how many tactical victories the enemy won, the will of the Italic people could not be broken. Later the Romans saved Punic occupied Spain and Sicily. The great Roman commander Scipio brought the war to the enemy's land and defeated them.

Over the years that followed, the Roman Empire kept Europe safe, but later when the Empire became weak and then fell apart, the Asiatic Huns attacked us from the East in 372 AD. Attila came in 451 AD leading an army that destroyed almost everything in its path.

In 711 AD the Afro-Arab Moors invaded the Iberian Peninsula from the south. They took our land and occupied it for hundreds of years. Only the Franks stopped them from taking France.

The Europeans had to fight the Moors for every inch of our people's land we slowly got back. We had to fight the Mongols too when they were led by Batu Khan in 1239 AD. The Mongols were finally driven out of Europe by the Duke of Muscovy in 1480 and the last Moorish kingdom on our land was destroyed by Spanish soldiers in 1492. We also had to fight the Turks who attacked us in the 14th century. A united army of our European peoples stopped them at the Gates of Vienna, but it took another few hundred years to get back the land they occupied and they still control a small piece of our land today!

Our most dangerous enemies today are the Jews who control our school and media. They are always teaching us about all the so-called "crimes" our people are guilty of. They then use this "White guilt" to get us to go along with opening our lands up to the same peoples who have been attacking us for thousands of years. Our enemies know in Mother Nature's war for survival it's us or them, but our people are being tricked to believe we can share our food and land with other peoples. Our great people are slowly dying because of this.

Our White peoples have had some very hard times. We have been through just as much as any other people. Our peoples had to fight in wars that were sometimes hopeless. They fought to the death in some battles just so their loved ones could have time to get away to safety. Today we are being taught lies from the people who control our schools and media. We are now slowly dying from laws and social policies that favor other peoples more than our own. They have created a poison called "White guilt" by only teaching us about all the so-called crimes we have done to others. We need to teach our people about our struggles so they will know that they have nothing to be sorry for.

RaHoWa!